VOYAGES OF DISCOVERY

Exploring
AFRICA

Editor April McCroskie

Illustrated by Gerald Wood

Produced by The Salariya Book Company Ltd
25, Marlborough Place, Brighton, England

© The Salariya Book Company Ltd

Published by
PETER BEDRICK BOOKS
2112 Broadway
New York, NY 10023

Library of Congress
Cataloging-in-Publication Data

Martell, Hazel
Exploring Africa / Hazel Mary Martell, Gerald
Wood.
p. cm. — (Voyages of discovery)
Includes index
ISBN 0-87226-490-4
1. Africa—Discovery and exploration–Juvenile lit-
erature. I. Wood, Gerald. II. Title. III. Series.
DT3 M43 1997
960—dc21   97–15230
                                 CIP

Printed in Hong Kong
First edition, 1997

Exploring
AFRICA

Hazel Mary Martell   Gerald Wood

PETER BEDRICK BOOKS

NEW YORK

CONTENTS

The border design is
based on the painted walls
of the huts of the Ndebele tribe
of the Transvaal, South Africa.

INTRODUCTION

Africa is the second-largest continent in the world and covers an area of nearly 12 million square miles. It is roughly triangular in shape, with the Mediterranean Sea to the north, the Atlantic Ocean to the west and the Indian Ocean to the east. It is also linked by land to Arabia in the north-east.

Evidence from Laetoli in Tanzania shows that human-like creatures, called Australopithecines, were living there almost 4 million years ago. Around 2.4 million years later a species called Homo erectus, or "upright human", appeared. These were the direct ancestors of modern humans. They could make tools, fire, and clothes from animal skins. This allowed them to become the first explorers of Africa because they were able to move away from the hot, dry climate of the savanna lands and populate the rest of the continent. It is likely that they eventually reached Asia and Europe, before being replaced by Homo sapiens around 400,000 years ago.

In more recent times, most of the people who have explored Africa have come from outside the continent. The Phoenicians and the Romans built towns to the north of the Sahara Desert, and explored parts of the coastline. Later the Vikings visited the north coast and traded for slaves, while Arab traders crossed the Sahara, taking with them their Islamic faith. Inside Africa itself, great kingdoms and empires flourished at various times. They included Ghana and Songhai, Great Zimbabwe and Ashanti, all of whose wealth came from trade.

Then, from the 15th century onwards, Europeans began to explore Africa more seriously. Some went as traders and some as missionaries. Others set out along the Nile, Niger, Zaire and Zambezi rivers to find out more about the interior of the continent, its peoples and its animal and plant life.

Unfortunately, some Europeans thought they were superior to the Africans and forced many of them into slavery, while European rulers began to take control of the continent and divide its lands amongst themselves. By 1900 only Liberia and Ethiopia were still independent.

This book tells you more about the explorers and their journeys. It also tells you more about the Africa they explored and about the effect they had on the continent.

Africa Before AD 1500

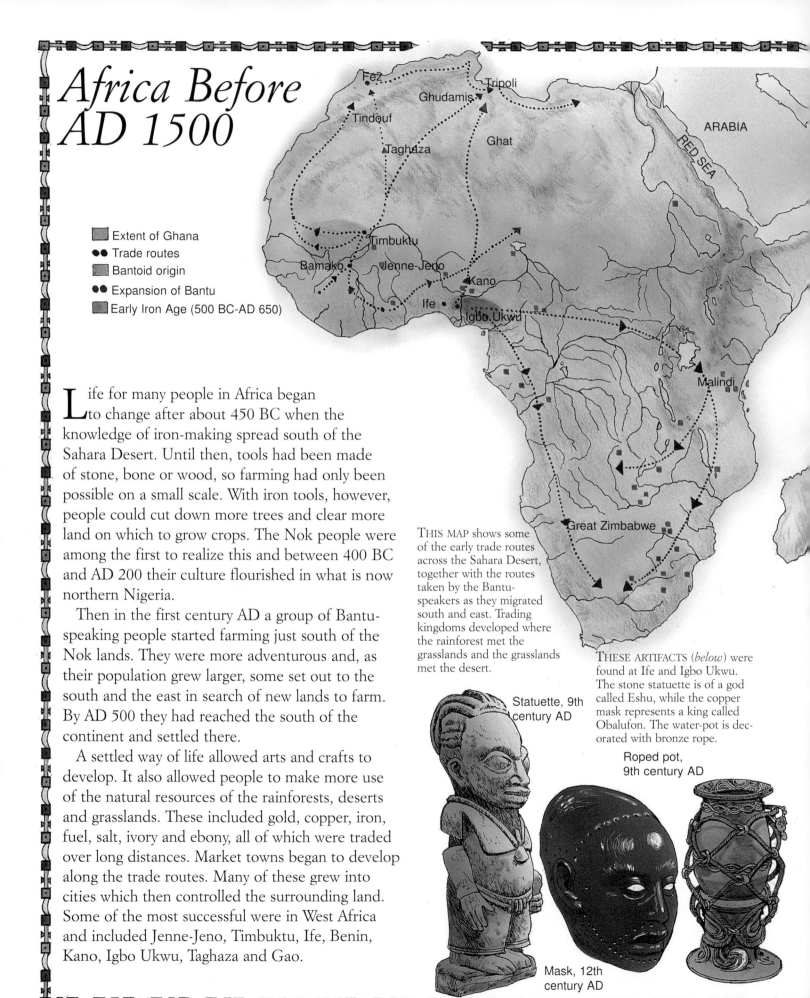

Extent of Ghana
Trade routes
Bantoid origin
Expansion of Bantu
Early Iron Age (500 BC–AD 650)

Fez
Tripoli
Ghudamis
Tindouf
Ghat
Taghaza
ARABIA
RED SEA
Timbuktu
Bamako
Jenne-Jeno
Kano
Ife
Igbo Ukwu
Malindi
Great Zimbabwe

Life for many people in Africa began to change after about 450 BC when the knowledge of iron-making spread south of the Sahara Desert. Until then, tools had been made of stone, bone or wood, so farming had only been possible on a small scale. With iron tools, however, people could cut down more trees and clear more land on which to grow crops. The Nok people were among the first to realize this and between 400 BC and AD 200 their culture flourished in what is now northern Nigeria.

Then in the first century AD a group of Bantu-speaking people started farming just south of the Nok lands. They were more adventurous and, as their population grew larger, some set out to the south and the east in search of new lands to farm. By AD 500 they had reached the south of the continent and settled there.

A settled way of life allowed arts and crafts to develop. It also allowed people to make more use of the natural resources of the rainforests, deserts and grasslands. These included gold, copper, iron, fuel, salt, ivory and ebony, all of which were traded over long distances. Market towns began to develop along the trade routes. Many of these grew into cities which then controlled the surrounding land. Some of the most successful were in West Africa and included Jenne-Jeno, Timbuktu, Ife, Benin, Kano, Igbo Ukwu, Taghaza and Gao.

THIS MAP shows some of the early trade routes across the Sahara Desert, together with the routes taken by the Bantu-speakers as they migrated south and east. Trading kingdoms developed where the rainforest met the grasslands and the grasslands met the desert.

THESE ARTIFACTS (*below*) were found at Ife and Igbo Ukwu. The stone statuette is of a god called Eshu, while the copper mask represents a king called Obalufon. The water-pot is decorated with bronze rope.

Statuette, 9th century AD

Roped pot, 9th century AD

Mask, 12th century AD

THE BANTU-SPEAKERS left the rainforests and the deserts to peoples who lived by hunting and gathering, or by grazing cattle. The Bantu-speakers moved to areas where the land was suitable for farming.

ONCE THEY FOUND a place to settle, they built villages of dome-shaped houses. Each house was made of a wooden frame covered with dried grass. This was then plastered inside and out with a layer of clay.

THEY CHOPPED DOWN trees to make room for farming. Some of the wood was used for fuel and some for building. The rest was burned where it fell and the ashes from it were dug into the soil to make it more fertile.

AROUND THEIR VILLAGES the Bantu-speakers grew cereal crops and kept herds of sheep, goats and cattle. They also smelted iron for tools and weapons, and made pots for storage and cooking.

A Bantu settlement.

IRON was often smelted in a dome-shaped furnace made from clay. Clay pipes, called tuyeres, were built into the walls at the level of the fire. Bellows were used to force air through the tuyeres and make the fire burn hot enough to turn the iron ore into metal.

THESE ARTIFACTS are from east Africa. The soapstone figures are from Great Zimbabwe, while the pot is from Kilwa on the coast. The wooden-handled pick would be used, before seeds were sown, to break up hard lumps in the soil.

Statuette, 13th-14th century

Pot, 14th century

Pick with iron head

Bird-like figure, 13th-14th century

In east Africa cities grew up along the coast as trade with the Arab world expanded. In their markets, silk and porcelain from China, spices from India, and glass beads from Arabia were exchanged for ivory, gold, tortoiseshell and slaves from inland cities such as Great Zimbabwe.

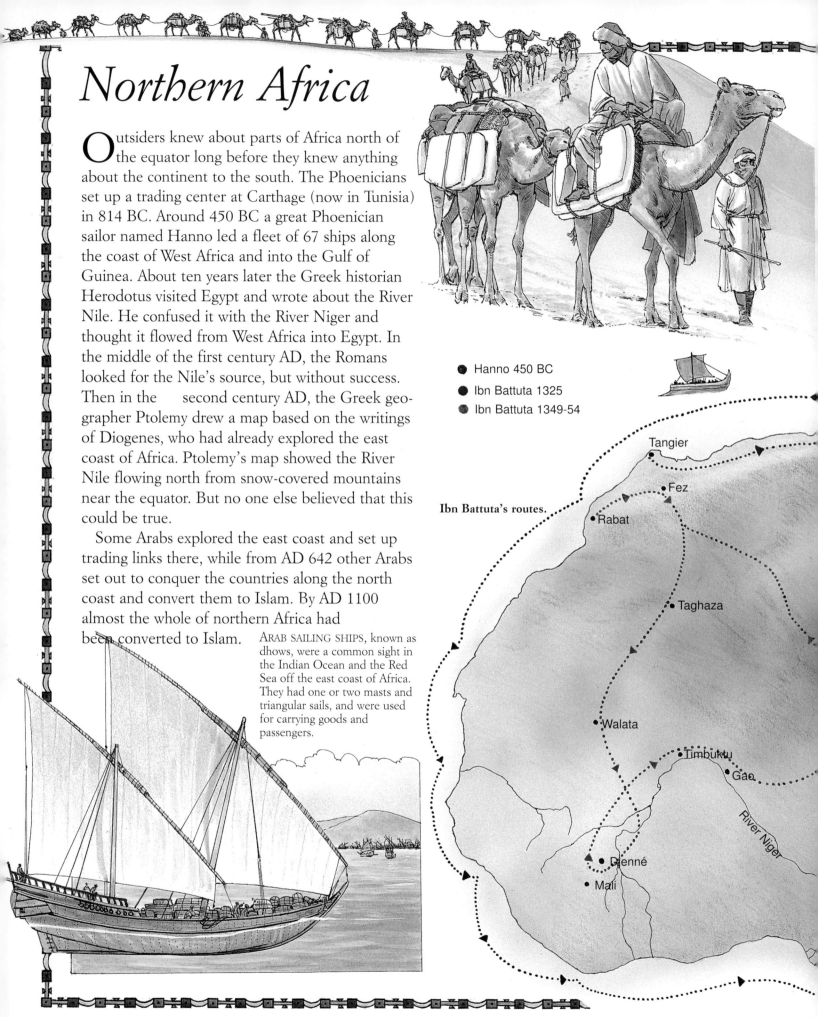

Northern Africa

Outsiders knew about parts of Africa north of the equator long before they knew anything about the continent to the south. The Phoenicians set up a trading center at Carthage (now in Tunisia) in 814 BC. Around 450 BC a great Phoenician sailor named Hanno led a fleet of 67 ships along the coast of West Africa and into the Gulf of Guinea. About ten years later the Greek historian Herodotus visited Egypt and wrote about the River Nile. He confused it with the River Niger and thought it flowed from West Africa into Egypt. In the middle of the first century AD, the Romans looked for the Nile's source, but without success. Then in the second century AD, the Greek geographer Ptolemy drew a map based on the writings of Diogenes, who had already explored the east coast of Africa. Ptolemy's map showed the River Nile flowing north from snow-covered mountains near the equator. But no one else believed that this could be true.

Some Arabs explored the east coast and set up trading links there, while from AD 642 other Arabs set out to conquer the countries along the north coast and convert them to Islam. By AD 1100 almost the whole of northern Africa had been converted to Islam.

ARAB SAILING SHIPS, known as dhows, were a common sight in the Indian Ocean and the Red Sea off the east coast of Africa. They had one or two masts and triangular sails, and were used for carrying goods and passengers.

- ● Hanno 450 BC
- ● Ibn Battuta 1325
- ● Ibn Battuta 1349–54

Ibn Battuta's routes.

Tangier
Fez
Rabat
Taghaza
Walata
Timbuktu
Gao
Djenné
Mali
River Niger

THIS CHURCH at Lalibela in Ethiopia was cut into solid rock. In the Middle Ages legend grew about a Christian king called Prester John who was supposed to live there. Explorers and Papal emissaries were sent to find him.

THE CAMEL was the ideal beast for crossing the Sahara Desert. It could travel long distances without needing much water and its large, flat feet stopped it sinking into soft sand. There were often 1000 or more camels in a camel train.

THIS MAP OF THE WORLD was drawn by Al Idrisi who was born in North Africa around AD 1100. It shows a source for the River Nile which is quite near to the actual one.

IBN BATTUTA was one of the greatest of all the Muslim travelers. He was born in Tangier in 1304 and traveled nearly 100,000 miles before his death in 1377.

Arabs set up long trade routes across the Sahara Desert. Salt, weapons and cloth were exchanged for gold, ivory and slaves. As well as trading, some Arabs traveled simply to gain more knowledge. They wrote accounts of their journeys, some of which can still be read today.

THE MOSQUE at Djenné was first built in the 14th century from mud-bricks. These have since been replaced many times, but the appearance of the mosque is the same as when it was first built.

Tripoli

Alexandria

Cairo

Jerusalem

Euphrates

Tabriz

Isfahan

Shiraz

River Nile

Mecca

Jedda

Aden

Mogadishu

9

Southern Africa

Although Europeans had been aware of Africa's vast resources for centuries, they made no serious attempts at sailing along its west coast until the first half of the 15th century. By this time, Europe had recovered from the ravages of the Black Death which had killed vast numbers of people between 1347 and 1348. Trade and agriculture had picked up again and many countries were beginning to grow wealthy. They began to look for new markets where they could sell the goods they produced in exchange for luxury items which were not easily available to them.

They also thought it might be possible to sail around Africa to reach India and the Far East to buy spices directly from the growers. Spices were necessary in medieval cooking because there was no refrigeration to keep meat fresh. It had to be salted, smoked or dried to try and preserve it. Even then it was usually going bad by the time it was cooked, so spices were added to hide the rotten taste. Most spices were traded through Constantinople (modern Istanbul), but in 1453 the city became part of the Ottoman Empire and European traders were no longer welcome. This made the search for a new trade route more urgent. But Bartolomeu Dias, the first European to sail around the tip of Africa into the Indian Ocean, did not make it until 1488.

THE SPICES the Europeans wanted included cardamom, cinnamon, cloves, ginger, mace, nutmeg, pepper and turmeric. They were grown in parts of India, Sri Lanka and the islands we now call Indonesia.

ONCE THEY had found their way through the Indian Ocean, the Portuguese controlled the spice trade for about 100 years. After 1600, however, the Dutch and the British were also involved.

Many of the later explorers who made their way inland along the great rivers were also motivated by the need for trade, as well as by a sense of adventure. Others were Christian missionaries who wanted to spread their religion among the Africans. By the end of the 19th century, however, there was a new sort of explorer in Africa. Often sent out by European rulers, these people planned to set up trading links. But as a result of claiming various areas, these explorers divided up the whole continent among the European powers.

TRADE between Africa and China was already established by the time the Europeans sailed into the Indian Ocean. Chinese pottery has been found in the ruins of Great Zimbabwe, (*left*) a town which flourished in the late 14th century then fell into a sharp decline after 1440.

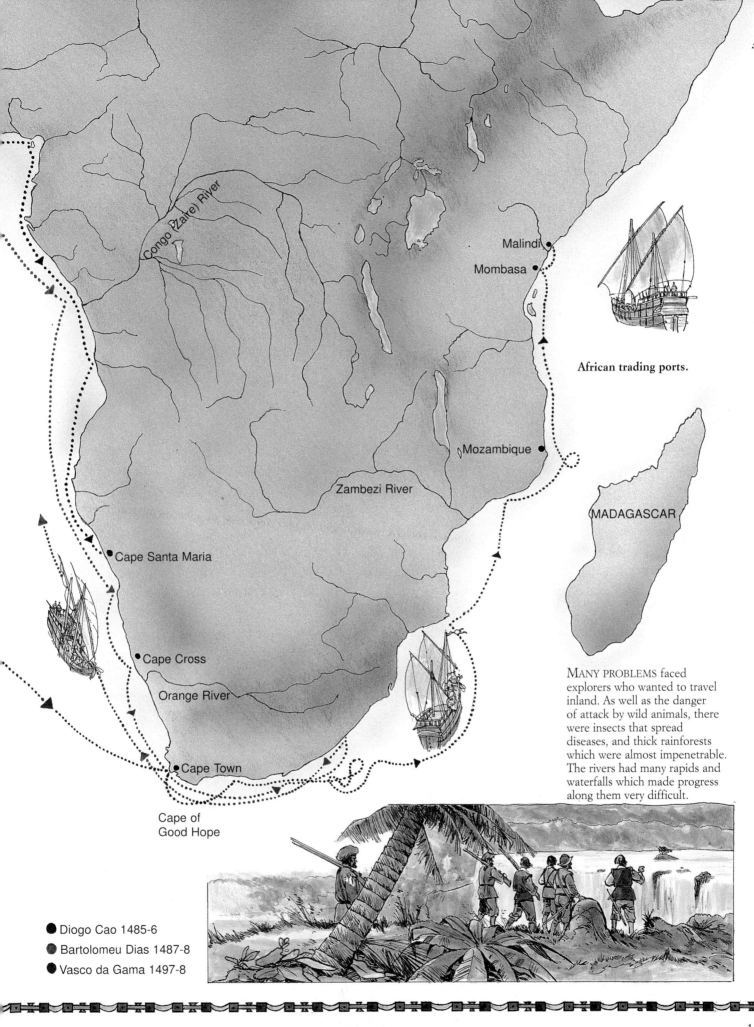

Congo (Zaire) River

Malindi

Mombasa

African trading ports.

Mozambique

Zambezi River

MADAGASCAR

Cape Santa Maria

Cape Cross

Orange River

MANY PROBLEMS faced
explorers who wanted to travel
inland. As well as the danger
of attack by wild animals, there
were insects that spread
diseases, and thick rainforests
which were almost impenetrable.
The rivers had many rapids and
waterfalls which made progress
along them very difficult.

Cape Town

Cape of
Good Hope

● Diogo Cao 1485-6

● Bartolomeu Dias 1487-8

● Vasco da Gama 1497-8

Portuguese Exploration

European exploration of Africa began around 1415 when Prince Henry of Portugal helped to capture the city of Ceuta (now in Morocco) from the Muslims. The city was a great trading center for gold, ivory and other valuable goods which were brought across the Sahara Desert from the region of the Senegal River in West Africa. In 1418 Henry started to sponsor expeditions to see if this river could be reached by sea.

In 1419 Henry set up his own court at Sagres in southern Portugal, and by 1424 he was ready to send out more expeditions to explore the west coast of Africa. In the next 10 years, 14 expeditions set out but they all turned back before they reached Cape Bojador. This was partly because many sailors believed the earth was flat and were afraid they would fall over the edge if they went further.

When the 15th expedition, led by Gil Eanes, reached Cape Bojador and returned safely in 1434, sailors were encouraged to venture further south. They were encouraged again after 1441 when a ship returned with gold and slaves from the West African coast. This was the start of European involvement in the slave trade and by 1448 it was already on a scale large enough for Henry to build a fort and a trading post on Arguin Island near Cape Blanco.

DIOGO CAO set up a stone pillar, called a padrao, at each place he landed on the coast of Africa. As well as the cross on the top, each padrao had the coat-of-arms of the Portuguese king, John II.

THE PORTUGUESE sailed in sturdy wooden ships called caravels. They were about 65 feet long and carried a crew of around 25 men. It often took a year or more to plan and organize an expedition.

When Henry died in 1460, Portuguese sailors had reached the coast of Sierra Leone. Most of them wanted to make a quick profit from trade, then sail back to Portugal as soon as possible. But the first true explorer appeared in the 1480s. Called Diogo Cao, he sailed further south than anyone else, and recorded what he saw on his journeys. In 1482 he reached the mouth of the Congo River (now the Zaire River) and in 1485 he reached Cape Cross in what is now Namibia.

FRIGHTENED SAILORS claimed that the ocean smoked and boiled in the region of Cape Bojador. What they probably saw were banks of fog and the effects of volcanic eruptions which we now know take place on the ocean floor.

PRINCE HENRY (*right*) was born in Portugal in 1394. His mother was English, so England and Portugal were close allies at this time. Henry was a soldier, not a sailor, and never went on any voyages of discovery. He was called Henry the Navigator, however, because of the encouragement he gave to other explorers.

A caravel.

SAILORS in the 15th century thought the seas were full of monsters and sea-serpents which could easily crush or capsize a ship. It is more likely that what they actually saw were large whales, porpoises swimming in a line, and large rafts of seaweed which were partly underwater.

AFTER SAILING round Cape Bojador, Gil Eanes went ashore and gathered some samples of plants to take back to Portugal. They included this flower, called the Saint Mary's rose, and helped to convince people that they were not going to sail into the mouth of hell.

Into the Indian Ocean

In 1488 Portuguese captain, Bartolomeu Dias, became the first European to sail around the Cape of Good Hope and into the Indian Ocean. His journey was sponsored by King John II of Portugal, who wanted Dias to find the southern limit of Africa and see if it was possible to sail around it to India.

Dias probably left Lisbon, Portugal, in August 1487 with three ships. By December he had sailed further south along the coast than Cao had done, but violent storms forced him out into the open sea. He continued south until the storms died down, then turned east. With no coastline in sight, he turned north and eventually landed at a place called Mossel Bay. He had sailed round the Cape of Good Hope without seeing it. He then sailed on up the coast to Algoa Bay, before his weary crew forced him to turn back.

Once Dias had proved it was possible to sail around Africa, plans were made to send an expedition from Portugal to India to try and set up a direct trading link between the two countries. It was led by Vasco da Gama and set out in 1497. By Christmas Day he had sailed further than Dias and landed on the coast of what he called Natal.

EARLY EXPLORERS found what latitude they were at by using an astrolabe to measure the height of the sun above the horizon at midday.

THE COMPASS always pointed to magnetic north so that explorers could use it to find out in which direction they were traveling.

A CROSS-STAFF was used to check on the position of the stars. Sailors could then work out how far north or south they were. But if it was cloudy they could go off course easily.

THIS MAP (*below*) shows the routes taken by Dias, da Gama and Cabral. Da Gama's journey back from India to Africa took four months as he had to keep zigzagging against the wind.

AFTER ROUNDING the Cape of Good Hope, da Gama made landfall in Mossel Bay. He traded with the Hottentot peoples for an ox, but then quarreled with them after his crew stole their water.

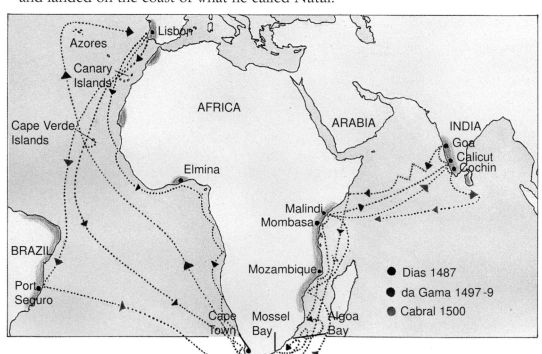

Lisbon
Azores
Canary Islands
Cape Verde Islands
AFRICA
ARABIA
INDIA
Goa
Calicut
Cochin
Elmina
Malindi
Mombasa
BRAZIL
Mozambique
Port Seguro
Cape Town
Mossel Bay
Algoa Bay

● Dias 1487
● da Gama 1497-9
● Cabral 1500

Bartolomeu Dias sails around the Cape of Good Hope.

SAILING AROUND the Cape of Good Hope was extremely dangerous for a small ship. It was nearly always stormy, with gale-force winds whipping up the ocean into huge waves. Although Bartolomeu Dias sailed around it safely in 1488, Cabral's expedition was not so lucky and he lost four ships there on his outward journey.

Da Gama continued up the coast to Mozambique, Mombasa and Malindi, from where an Arab pilot showed him how to take advantage of the monsoon winds for the crossing to India. He reached Calicut in May 1498, only to find that trade there was in the hands of Muslim merchants who were reluctant to share it with the newcomers.

Da Gama returned to Lisbon, but in March 1500 another expedition, led by Pedro Alvarez Cabral, set out to make the same journey. To avoid the rough seas and bad currents on the journey south, Cabral sailed far to the west of Africa and landed briefly on the coast of Brazil. He claimed the whole of the country for Portugal, then continued the journey to India, which he reached in September.

BARTOLOMEU DIAS was born in Portugal in 1450. Very little is known of his early life, except that he held a lowly rank in the royal household. He was captain of one of the ships which sailed with Cabral in 1500 and was drowned at sea when it was wrecked off the Cape.

Trade with India

Vasco da Gama failed to set up a trade link with India on his first visit as the goods he had taken with him were not of a high enough value to impress the Muslim ruler of Calicut. In 1500, however, Cabral fared a little better. When he arrived in September, the ruler allowed him to set up a fortified trading post. This led to problems with the other traders and in December they attacked the Portuguese post and killed many of the people in it. In revenge, Cabral bombarded the city from his ships in the harbor. He captured 10 ships belonging to Muslim traders and killed their crews. After that, he visited the ports of Cochin, Caranglos and Cannanore where he traded for spices before returning to Portugal.

Following Cabral's success, the king of Portugal sent a new fleet of ships to India under Vasco da Gama's command. They left Lisbon in February 1502 and reached the coast of East Africa in June. They visited Mozambique and Kilwa, where da Gama threatened to burn the town unless the ruler agreed to be ruled by the Portuguese. The fleet sailed on to Goa and then Cannanore, where da Gama captured an Arab ship and stole its cargo. He then trapped around 300 passengers, and set fire to the ship.

VASCO DA GAMA (*left*) was born at Sines in Portugal around 1460. He was the son of a nobleman and in his youth he studied mathematics and navigation. In 1492 the king sent him to attack French ships off southern Portugal. He made three trips to India and died there in 1524.

THIS 16TH-CENTURY salt-cellar (*right*) was carved in Africa from ivory. It shows a Portuguese ship with its fierce-looking captain and his crew, all of whom are heavily armed. It was probably traded in exchange for weapons from Europe, or cloth from India or China.

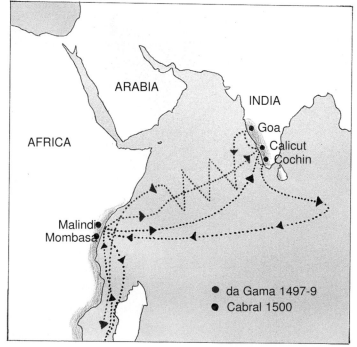

Map legend:
ARABIA
INDIA
AFRICA
Goa
Calicut
Cochin
Malindi
Mombasa
● da Gama 1497-9
● Cabral 1500

THE PORTUGUESE set up a string of trading posts along the east coast of Africa, many of which had previously been controlled by the Arabs. Each one had a fort to defend it against the local people, and against any other traders who might try and take it over.

IN THE 16TH CENTURY the Europeans traded guns for cloth, and spices such as ginger, pepper, cloves and cinnamon. But in later centuries, they imported raw cotton from India, made it into cloth in Europe, then sold it back to the Indians at huge profits.

FORT JESUS was built in the late 16th century to protect the busy Portuguese trading colony at Mombasa. As well as stopping there to trade, many ships called in for supplies for the rest of the voyage, and for repairs. These repairs included careening, which involved sailing the ships onto the beach so that the shellfish which gathered on the underwater planks could be scraped off.

Loading supplies at Fort Jesus.

When da Gama reached Calicut, he ordered the ruler to banish the Muslim traders. To make sure he was obeyed, da Gama also bombarded the port, killed 38 fishermen who sailed out to trade with him, and destroyed much of the Arab fleet. These violent actions opened the way for the Portuguese to take over trade between India and Europe.

Control of this trade helped to make Portugal a very rich country in the 16th century. Later the Dutch, French and British also became involved, and trade wars often broke out between them. By the 18th century Britain dominated trade with India and also began to take control of the country itself.

The Slave Trade

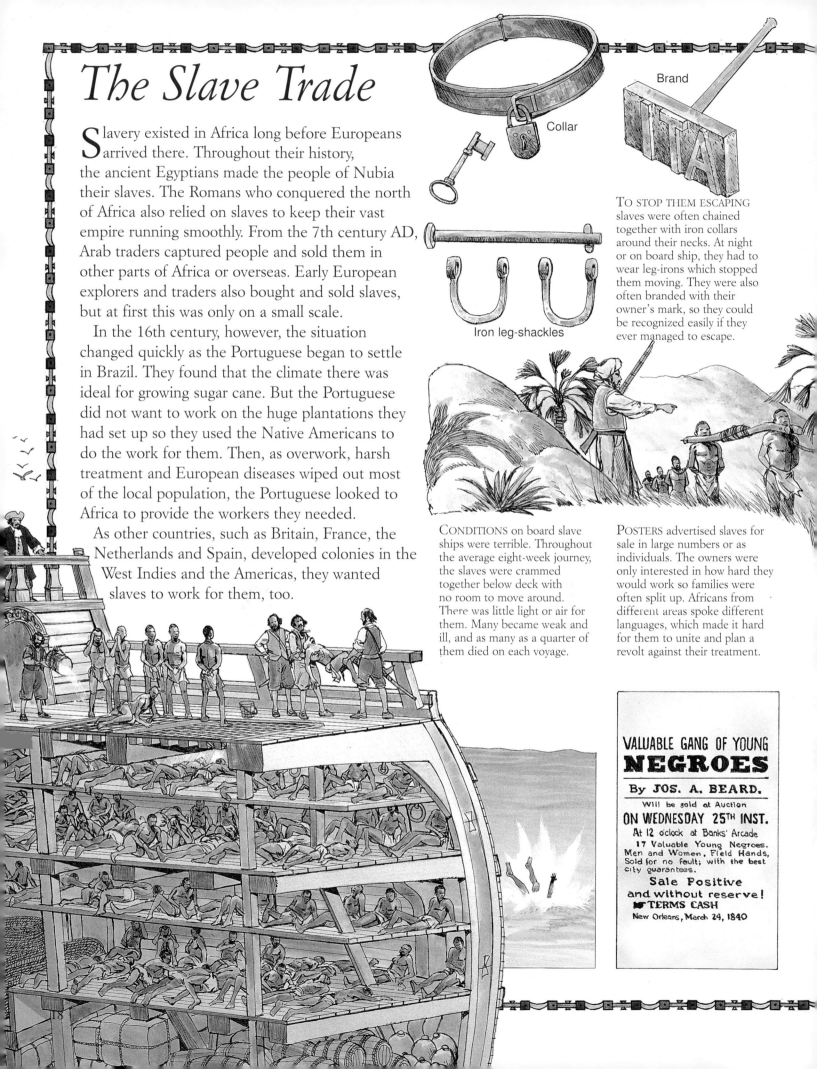

Slavery existed in Africa long before Europeans arrived there. Throughout their history, the ancient Egyptians made the people of Nubia their slaves. The Romans who conquered the north of Africa also relied on slaves to keep their vast empire running smoothly. From the 7th century AD, Arab traders captured people and sold them in other parts of Africa or overseas. Early European explorers and traders also bought and sold slaves, but at first this was only on a small scale.

In the 16th century, however, the situation changed quickly as the Portuguese began to settle in Brazil. They found that the climate there was ideal for growing sugar cane. But the Portuguese did not want to work on the huge plantations they had set up so they used the Native Americans to do the work for them. Then, as overwork, harsh treatment and European diseases wiped out most of the local population, the Portuguese looked to Africa to provide the workers they needed.

As other countries, such as Britain, France, the Netherlands and Spain, developed colonies in the West Indies and the Americas, they wanted slaves to work for them, too.

Collar

Brand

Iron leg-shackles

TO STOP THEM ESCAPING slaves were often chained together with iron collars around their necks. At night or on board ship, they had to wear leg-irons which stopped them moving. They were also often branded with their owner's mark, so they could be recognized easily if they ever managed to escape.

CONDITIONS on board slave ships were terrible. Throughout the average eight-week journey, the slaves were crammed together below deck with no room to move around. There was little light or air for them. Many became weak and ill, and as many as a quarter of them died on each voyage.

POSTERS advertised slaves for sale in large numbers or as individuals. The owners were only interested in how hard they would work so families were often split up. Africans from different areas spoke different languages, which made it hard for them to unite and plan a revolt against their treatment.

VALUABLE GANG OF YOUNG
NEGROES
By JOS. A. BEARD.
Will be sold at Auction
ON WEDNESDAY 25TH INST.
At 12 o'clock at Banks' Arcade
17 Valuable Young Negroes.
Men and Women, Field Hands.
Sold for no fault; with the best city guarantees.
**Sale Positive
and without reserve!**
TERMS CASH
New Orleans, March 24, 1840

ON PLANTATIONS slaves had to work very hard for long hours. They were housed badly, fed poorly and treated cruelly. They could be whipped or beaten, and many died as a result of their horrible treatment.

MANY SLAVES were taken from deep in the center of Africa. They were chained together and forced to march long distances to the ports where ships were waiting to take them across the Atlantic.

Slaves walking to a port.

SLAVERY was part of a profitable trade triangle. Slaves were traded in the Americas for sugar which was sent to Europe. The sugar was traded for guns and cloth which were sent to Africa and traded for more slaves.

Soon vast numbers of Africans were being captured from their homes and shipped across the Atlantic. At first they worked mainly on sugar plantations and on sugar-processing plants, but later they also worked on tobacco and cotton plantations further north.

In the 19th century reformers began to campaign against slavery, and in 1833 it was abolished in the British Empire. It was abolished in the USA in 1865 and in Brazil in 1889, by which time it is thought that around 20 million Africans had been forced from their homes and made into slaves.

Scientific Exploration

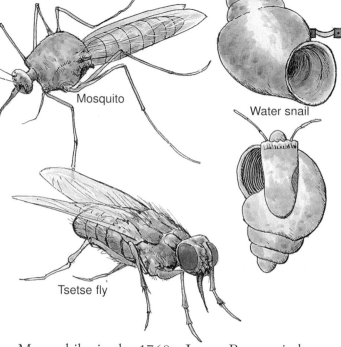

Mosquito

Water snail

Tsetse fly

At the start of the 18th century, Europeans still knew very little about Africa apart from the trading ports and the Dutch colony in Cape Town, which, since 1652, provided supplies for Dutch trading ships sailing to India and the East Indies. A fear of the unknown stopped Europeans going any further inland as they thought the way would be blocked by thick rainforests, huge deserts, fierce wild animals, poisonous snakes and deadly diseases.

By the middle of the century, however, some people in Europe were beginning to take a more serious interest in science and in the world about them. Ships which set out to explore the islands of the Pacific Ocean took botanists and zoologists with them to study the local plants and animals. One of the botanists who sailed with Captain Cook in 1768 was Joseph Banks. Twenty years later he founded the Association for Promoting the Discovery of the Interior Parts of Africa (more usually known as the African Association). Its first aim was to find the River Niger and the city of Timbuktu, both of which had been visited by the Arab traveler, Ibn Battuta, in 1335 (*see pages 8-9*).

Meanwhile, in the 1760s, James Bruce tried to find the source of the River Nile. He prepared for the journey by studying Spanish, Portuguese and Arabic, and wore Arab dress when he travelled through Egypt. Having reached Aswan, he made his way to the Red Sea coast then sailed to Ethiopia. From the coast, he went overland to the capital, Gondar, and then on to Lake Tana. There he followed a river which fed into the lake and, when he reached its source, he was convinced that this was the source of the Nile. In fact he had found the source of the Blue Nile (or Bahr el-Azrak) which is the main tributary of the River Nilc.

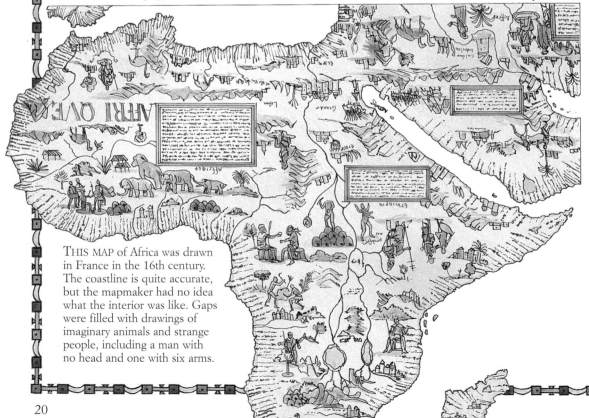

THIS MAP of Africa was drawn in France in the 16th century. The coastline is quite accurate, but the mapmaker had no idea what the interior was like. Gaps were filled with drawings of imaginary animals and strange people, including a man with no head and one with six arms.

JAMES BRUCE was a Scottish landowner who served as British consul in Algiers from 1763. He set out from Alexandria in July 1768 and reached Lake Tana in November 1770. He later retired to his estate in Scotland and wrote a book about his travels.

IN AFRICA it was not just the big animals that Europeans had to be scared of. Away from the coast, there were mosquitoes which could pass on the disease malaria in their bite, and tsetse flies which could pass on sleeping sickness in the same way. Water snails carried the larvae of a flatworm called bilharzia. These larvae could pass through the skin of anyone who came into contact with infected water and could cause severe problems in the intestine or the bladder. All these infections were life-threatening.

James Bruce drinks a toast.

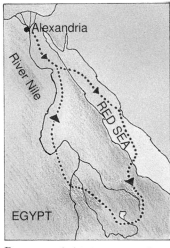

BRUCE made his journey partly by river, partly by sea and partly by land. His journey home was more difficult than his outward one had been and he did not reach Marseilles in southern France until March 1773. He finally returned to London the following year.

THIS PICTURE (*above*) is based on a contemporary drawing of James Bruce drinking a toast from what he thought was the source of the Nile. He dedicated his achievement to the British king, George III. To his dismay, however, he found that at least two other Europeans had been there before him. Francisco Alvarez and Pedro Paez were two Jesuit priests who had explored the area at least a century before.

BRUCE'S BOOK, *Travels to Discover the Source of the Nile*, was published in 1790. As well as detailed descriptions of the people of Ethiopia, their life and their customs, the book contained illustrations of the many different plants and animals Bruce came across on his journey.

The River Niger

The African Association's first choice to explore the River Niger was John Ledyard, an American who had sailed with Captain Cook. He planned to travel overland from Egypt to Timbuktu, but died of dysentery soon after arriving in Cairo. Then the Association sent Daniel Houghton, a British Army officer. He landed at the mouth of the River Gambia and planned to travel east to Timbuktu, but was murdered by Muslims shortly afterwards.

In May 1795 Mungo Park was the third explorer to be sent to Africa. He arrived at Pisania on the Gambia River in July, but he caught a fever and was delayed for several months. He spent his time learning the local language and finding out more about the areas he was going to explore. In December he started out for the interior with two African companions. But the group was soon captured by a Muslim tribe and taken to Benown on the edge of the desert.

After three months, Park managed to escape and eventually reached the River Niger at Ségou. From there he traveled to Silla, but had to turn back because of bad weather and illness. It took him a year to make his way back to Pisania.

MUNGO PARK was born in Selkirk, Scotland in 1771. He had been to Sumatra, Indonesia, on an East India Company ship. There, he discovered eight new species of fish and wrote an article about them for a scientific journal in London. Joseph Banks read this article and was so impressed by it that he invited Park to explore the River Niger.

WHEN HE SET OUT from Pisania, Park took with him a compass and a pocket sextant like this one to help him find his way. He also took a thermometer, firearms, an umbrella, tobacco, beads and amber with which he could barter for food and provisions.

HAVING ESCAPED from Benown with nothing but his horse, Park nearly died of hunger and thirst. Then he met up with a party of refugees who were going to the market town of Ségou on the River Niger. He traveled with them for two weeks and on July 20 he finally caught his first glimpse of the river he had set out to find.

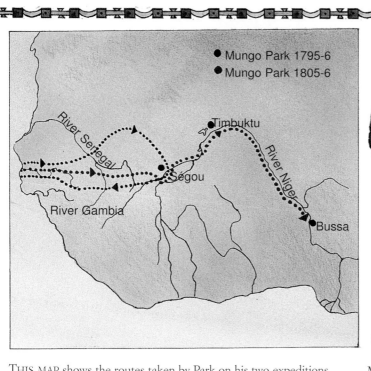

THIS MAP shows the routes taken by Park on his two expeditions to Africa. Before he set sail, no one in Europe knew where to find either the source or the mouth of the River Niger, or even the direction in which it flowed. From the writings of Ibn Battuta they knew that it flowed near the city of Timbuktu, but they thought it must be a tributary of the Nile.

MUNGO PARK was the first European man that the Muslim women of Benown had ever seen so they were as curious about him as he was about them. They were intrigued by his pale skin and thought he must have been washed in milk as a child to make it so white. They were also fascinated by the size of his nose and asked him if it had been pinched and pulled every day to make it so long.

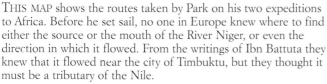

Park sees the River Niger for the first time.

Park led another expedition which arrived in The Gambia in May 1805 and reached Bamako on the Niger in August. By then most of the party had died, but those who were left went to Sansanding. There they made a boat which they called the *HMS Joliba* (after the local name for the Niger) and set off downstream. In 1806 their boat got stuck at the falls at Bussa and was attacked by locals. Panicking, Park and his four remaining companions jumped overboard to escape, but instead they all drowned.

The Sahara Desert

The Sahara Desert was a great problem to Europeans who wanted to explore the interior of North Africa. The only way they could cross it was by traveling with a caravan of Arab traders, but this was dangerous as the Arabs did not trust the Europeans and thought they would try and take over their trade.

The place that Europeans most wanted to visit was the city of Timbuktu. They had read of its grandeur in the writings of Ibn Battuta and believed it would be a place of great wealth and learning. It was also a place from which more of the River Niger could be explored.

The first European to set foot in the city was the Scottish explorer Alexander Laing who arrived on August 18, 1826. He left on September 24, but was murdered two days later by the man in charge of the caravan he was traveling with. Around this time, the French Geographical Society offered a prize for the first European to reach Timbuktu and return alive. René-Auguste Caillié, a Frenchman who had already visited Senegal, decided to try.

ALEXANDER GORDON LAING was born in Scotland in 1793. He served in the British Army in Senegal from where he visited what is now Sierra Leone. He started his journey to Timbuktu in July 1825 from Tripoli in Libya and spent over a year crossing the Sahara Desert.

RENÉ-AUGUSTE CAILLIÉ was born in France in 1799 and was the son of a baker. Fascinated by travelers' tales, he took a job as a servant on a ship when he was 16 and sailed to Senegal. Caillié had no financial backing and paid for his expeditions from his own savings.

Realizing he would be safer traveling as a Muslim, he spent several months in Senegal learning to speak Arabic and studying the Koran. Then, in March 1827, he traveled to the mouth of the Rio Nunez and, dressed as an Arab, he joined a salt caravan and started his journey. By June he had reached Kouroussa on the River Niger where he joined another caravan which was going to Djenné. He was taken ill at the town of Tieme, however, and had to stay there for five months.

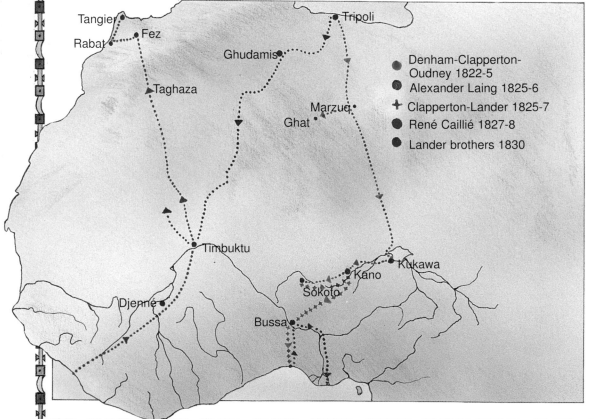

Denham-Clapperton-Oudney 1822-5
Alexander Laing 1825-6
Clapperton-Lander 1825-7
René Caillié 1827-8
Lander brothers 1830

Tangier, Rabat, Fez, Ghudamis, Tripoli, Taghaza, Marzuq, Ghat, Timbuktu, Kukawa, Kano, Sokoto, Djenné, Bussa

THIS MAP shows the routes taken by those exploring the Sahara Desert area. Laing and Caillie walked most of the way across the desert in temperatures which sometimes reached an incredible 160° F.

ON THE WAY Caillié suffered from malaria and scurvy and Laing was attacked by Tuareg tribesmen.

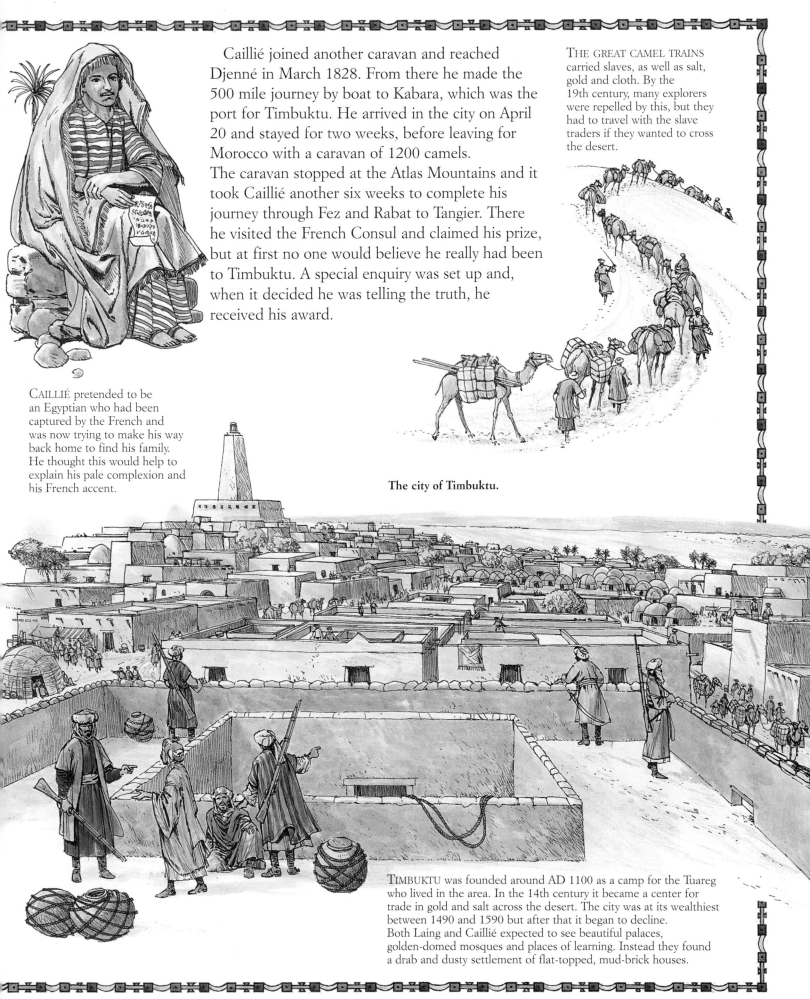

Caillié joined another caravan and reached Djenné in March 1828. From there he made the 500 mile journey by boat to Kabara, which was the port for Timbuktu. He arrived in the city on April 20 and stayed for two weeks, before leaving for Morocco with a caravan of 1200 camels. The caravan stopped at the Atlas Mountains and it took Caillié another six weeks to complete his journey through Fez and Rabat to Tangier. There he visited the French Consul and claimed his prize, but at first no one would believe he really had been to Timbuktu. A special enquiry was set up and, when it decided he was telling the truth, he received his award.

THE GREAT CAMEL TRAINS carried slaves, as well as salt, gold and cloth. By the 19th century, many explorers were repelled by this, but they had to travel with the slave traders if they wanted to cross the desert.

CAILLIÉ pretended to be an Egyptian who had been captured by the French and was now trying to make his way back home to find his family. He thought this would help to explain his pale complexion and his French accent.

The city of Timbuktu.

TIMBUKTU was founded around AD 1100 as a camp for the Tuareg who lived in the area. In the 14th century it became a center for trade in gold and salt across the desert. The city was at its wealthiest between 1490 and 1590 but after that it began to decline. Both Laing and Caillié expected to see beautiful palaces, golden-domed mosques and places of learning. Instead they found a drab and dusty settlement of flat-topped, mud-brick houses.

Barth and Richardson

After Caillié's journey to Timbuktu, other travelers from Europe tried to cross the Sahara to visit the cities on the southern edge of the desert. Most of them were unsuccessful and many died of disease or starvation along the route. Others were killed by the Tuareg or by powerful Arab merchants who were frightened of losing their control over trade across the desert.

Some travelers went out of curiosity and a sense of adventure, but others went to set up trade links with that part of Africa. Some also went to investigate Arab slave-trading with a view to stopping it. One of these was James Richardson who traveled on behalf of the British Bible Society. Leaving Tripoli in August 1845, he traveled to the oasis of Ghudamis and then to Ghat, before turning back to the Mediterranean coast. Although he only traveled about 700 miles into the desert, his account of the journey impressed people in Britain.

In 1850 the government appointed Richardson to lead an expedition from Tripoli to the far south of the Sahara. He took with him two Germans – Heinrich Barth, a scholar who spoke Arabic, and Adolf Overweg, a geologist.

HEINRICH BARTH was born in Germany, in 1821. He was a good linguist and was also more scientific and methodical than earlier explorers. Between 1845 and 1847 he traveled along the North African coast from Rabat to Alexandria, and in 1849 he published a book of his travels.

JAMES RICHARDSON did not try to hide his nationality or his religion. Instead, he traveled openly as a Christian and an Englishman. On his first visit to Ghat he was welcomed warmly by the local ruler who gave him presents to take back to Queen Victoria.

They set out in March 1850, taking with them guides and servants, plus large amounts of stores and equipment, scientific instruments and a large wooden boat.

Richardson and Barth soon found they could not get along with each other, but they traveled together to Ghat and then through the Tassili-n-Ajjer to Agadez. There they split up, with Richardson setting out to go directly to Lake Chad, while Overweg and Barth explored two more westerly routes. The three men agreed to meet again at Kukawa on the western shore of Lake Chad, but Richardson died there three weeks before Barth arrived.

BARTH reached Kano in February 1851. He found it was a beautiful and wealthy city of about 30,000 people. He urged the Europeans to set up trade links quickly as American slave-dealers were bringing in vast amounts of American goods to exchange for slaves.

WHEN RICHARDSON visited Africa, slavery had been abolished by Britain. But the slave trade continued with many Africans being captured and shipped off to the USA and parts of South America. Posters like this (*left*) reminded people of the situation and encouraged them to protest about it.

IN THE AREA of Tassili-n-Ajjer Barth saw rock carvings showing buffaloes and bulls. This led him to believe that the Sahara had not always been a desert and that these animals must once have been common. A hundred years later he was proved right when rock paintings showing giraffes, elephants, cattle, hippopotamuses and rhinoceroses were also found in the area.

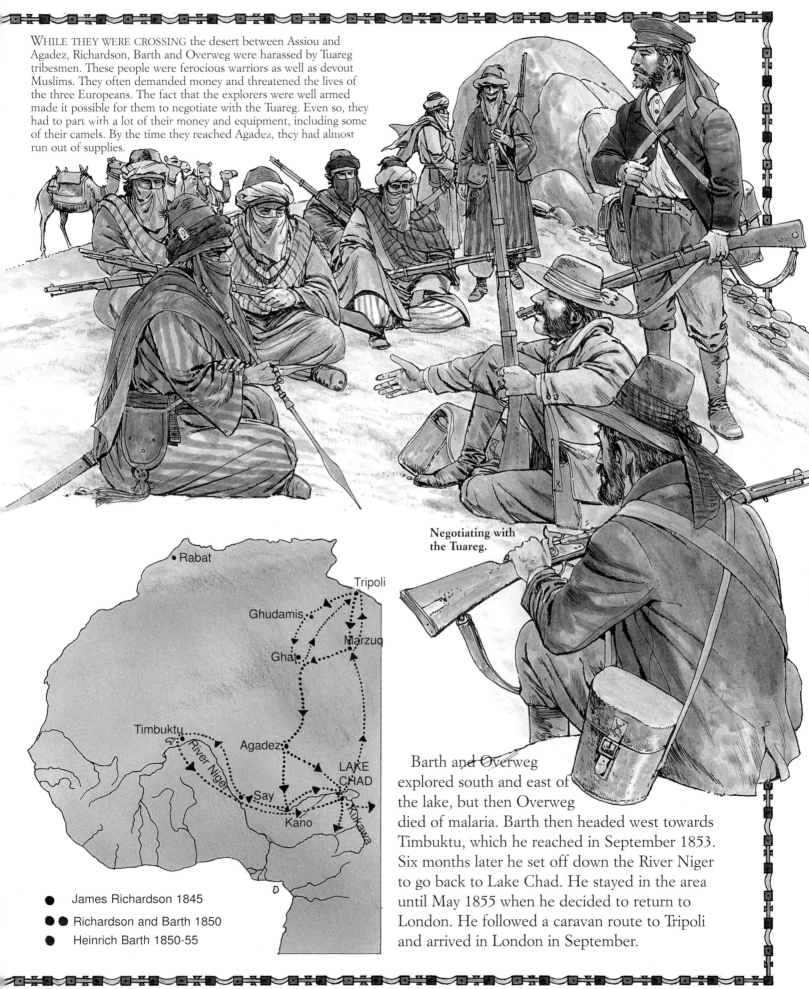

WHILE THEY WERE CROSSING the desert between Assiou and Agadez, Richardson, Barth and Overweg were harassed by Tuareg tribesmen. These people were ferocious warriors as well as devout Muslims. They often demanded money and threatened the lives of the three Europeans. The fact that the explorers were well armed made it possible for them to negotiate with the Tuareg. Even so, they had to part with a lot of their money and equipment, including some of their camels. By the time they reached Agadez, they had almost run out of supplies.

Negotiating with the Tuareg.

Barth and Overweg explored south and east of the lake, but then Overweg died of malaria. Barth then headed west towards Timbuktu, which he reached in September 1853. Six months later he set off down the River Niger to go back to Lake Chad. He stayed in the area until May 1855 when he decided to return to London. He followed a caravan route to Tripoli and arrived in London in September.

● James Richardson 1845

●● Richardson and Barth 1850

● Heinrich Barth 1850-55

The Source of the Nile

At the start of the 19th century, the source of the Nile had still not been found. Between 1820 and 1822 the viceroy of Egypt, Mohammed Ali Pasha, sent an expedition to explore the river. French explorer, Frederic Cailliaud, went with it as far as the junction of the Blue Nile and the White Nile, and made detailed drawings of all that he saw. The expedition itself went as far as Gondokoro.

The next people to try and find the source of the Nile were Richard Burton and John Speke from Britain. They arrived in Somalia in 1855 with two officers from the British East India Company. But their party was attacked, and both Speke and Burton were injured and had to return to England.

They made their second attempt in 1857. They were sponsored by the Royal Geographical Society in London which had taken over the exploration work of the former African Association. They left Bagamoyo on June 16, 1857 and followed a route normally used to take slaves and ivory to the coast. But the two leaders fell ill and had to stop at Kazeh (modern Tabora) until they recovered.

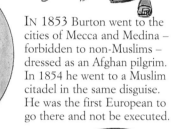

RICHARD BURTON liked unusual objects. His home from 1872 to 1890 was in Trieste, Italy, and was furnished in Middle-Eastern style, with much brassware and glass. This necklace of human bones was one of his strange souvenirs.

IN 1853 Burton went to the cities of Mecca and Medina – forbidden to non-Muslims – dressed as an Afghan pilgrim. In 1854 he went to a Muslim citadel in the same disguise. He was the first European to go there and not be executed.

JOHN HANNING SPEKE was born in England, in 1822. He became an officer in the British Indian Army in 1844. He served in the Punjab and spent some time exploring in the Himalayas and in Tibet. He had also studied botany and geology before going to Africa.

RICHARD BURTON was born in England in 1821, but spent his early years in France and Italy. He was a brilliant linguist who spoke over 30 languages. He traveled to many countries as a soldier, explorer and diplomat, and wrote 43 books about his travels. He died in 1890.

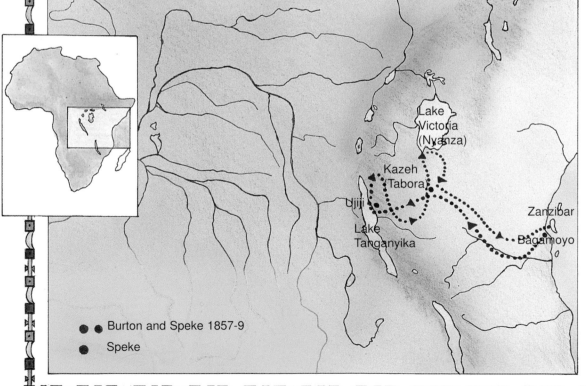

- ●● Burton and Speke 1857-9
- ● Speke

THIS MAP shows the routes taken by Burton and Speke in their search for the source of the Nile. They both agreed that Lake Tanganyika was not the source. Although Speke thought the source was in Lake Nyanza, Burton thought it would be in the direction of Mount Kilimanjaro.

At Kazeh an Arab advised them to go north towards Lake Nyanza, but Burton ignored his advice and headed west. On February 13, 1858 he and Speke became the first Europeans to see Lake Tanganyika. But again they fell ill and had to stop at a trading town called Ujiji from where they explored the north shore of the lake. Deciding that this was not the source of the Nile after all, they turned back to Kazeh. Burton was ill again so Speke set out alone to look for Lake Nyanza. He reached it on August 3, 1858 and, ignoring its African name, he called it Victoria after Queen Victoria of Britain.

Burton and Speke's camp.

THERE WERE ABOUT 100 porters on the expedition. They set up the camp at night and carried gifts to pay as tribute to local rulers. There was an armed escort of 30 men, and an Arab guide.

Speke was convinced that this was the source of the Nile and went back to Kazeh to tell Burton of his discovery. But Burton did not believe him and the two men quickly began to argue. Though they traveled together to Zanzibar, they split up there in February 1859 and Speke returned to London to tell the Royal Geographical Society of his discovery. Their great rivalry had begun.

MOST EXPLORERS wrote books about their travels when they returned home. Because photography was very new, they illustrated their books with pencil drawings and watercolors. Frederic Cailliaud included great detail of the clothes people wore, while John Speke made accurate drawings of animals, such as these white rhinoceroses.

WHITE RHINOCEROS

Speke and Grant

Speke

Grant

The quarrel between Speke and Burton continued when they were back in Britain. Other famous explorers started to take sides, until finally Speke decided to go on a second expedition to prove that he was right. He chose James Grant, a former army comrade to go with him.

They were sponsored by the Royal Geographical Society again and left Zanzibar in October 1860. They followed the same route to Kazeh that Speke had used in 1857 and then went on to Lake Victoria. There they split up. Grant went directly north to the kingdom of Bunyoro, while Speke went north along the eastern shore of the lake.

On 28 July 1862 Speke reached the northernmost end of the lake. There he found the great rapids he had been told about and named them the Ripon Falls, after a former-president of the Geographical Society. This was where the Nile left the lake, but although Speke wanted to do more exploring, he did not have time. Instead he had to meet Grant in Bunyoro, so that they could make their way back to Britain with the news. On the way they stopped at Gondokoro where they met Samuel and Florence Baker, who had been sent out to look for them.

SPEKE returned to England, but Burton was not convinced that Speke had found the source of the Nile. Burton claimed the source originated in a river flowing out of Lake Tanganyika. They arranged to meet and debate their theories at the Royal Geographical Society on September 16, 1864 but Speke died in a shooting accident the day before. Some people thought it may have been suicide because Speke was too scared to face Burton. If this is true then it is even more tragic as Speke's argument was right and Burton's was wrong.

BY 1863 SPEKE AND GRANT had been reported missing and Samuel Baker was sent out to look for them. After this meeting at Gondokoro, the Bakers decided they would also go exploring.

THE BAKERS became the first Europeans to see the Kabarega Falls, where the Victoria Nile drops to the level of Lake Luta Nzige. They decided to call the lake after Queen Victoria's husband, Albert, and called the falls after Roderick Murchison, who was then president of the Royal Geographical Society.

THIS MAP shows the routes followed by Speke, Grant and the Bakers as they looked for the source of the Nile. They did not realize that the Nile does not have just one source. Instead it has several different ones, some of which have only been mapped accurately in the 20th century.

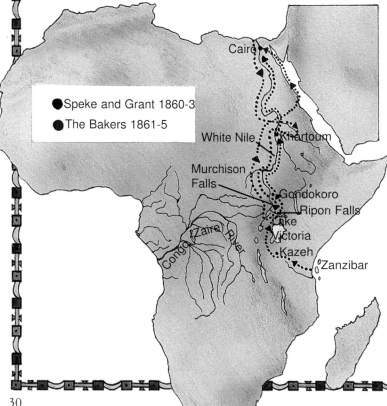

● Speke and Grant 1860-3
● The Bakers 1861-5

Cairo

White Nile
Khartoum
Murchison
Falls
Gondokoro
Ripon Falls
Lake
Victoria
Kazeh
Zanzibar
Congo (Zaire) River

FLORENCE BAKER was a Hungarian who had been taken prisoner by the Turks and put up for sale in a slave market. Samuel had seen her there and bought her in an auction. After that they were inseparable and traveled many thousands of miles together.

Grant joins in at a village festival.

MANY EXPLORERS, including Samuel Baker, thought they were superior to the people of Africa. But James Grant was interested in the people and in their country, and was willing to join in the dancing at their festivities.

THE ROYAL GEOGRAPHICAL SOCIETY gave Speke £2,000 (about $10,000 US) towards his second expedition. This meant that he was able to hire 26 porters to set out with him and Grant from Zanzibar. When they reached Lake Victoria, however, the number was down to 18. All the others had deserted as a result of the harsh conditions placed on them by the two leaders.

Livingstone and Stanley before 1856

David Livingstone and Henry Stanley were two of Africa's most famous explorers. Livingstone wanted to be a Christian missionary and Stanley was a journalist for the *New York Herald*. They first went to Africa as part of their work.

Livingstone arrived at Cape Colony in 1841 and made the 500 mile journey to Kuruman, a missionary post run by Robert Moffat. Livingstone spent some time there meeting the local people and learning their language, before going to Mabotsa to set up his own mission. He returned to Kuruman in 1844 to marry Mary Moffat. Together they set up a new mission at Kolobeng. But by 1848 Livingstone was dissatisfied with being a missionary so he joined an expedition across the Kalahari Desert. This expedition reached Lake Ngami then turned back.

He returned in 1851 and on August 4 he saw the Zambezi River for the first time. In June 1852 he set out to follow it from Shesheke to its source. He then spent two years traveling overland to Luanda on the Atlantic coast. He rested for a few months then headed back to Shesheke. He arrived in September 1855, then followed the river downstream. He eventually reached Quelimane on on May 25, 1856 after a journey of 5,600 miles.

THIS MAP shows Livingstone's journeys in Africa from 1841 to 1856. On these travels he was appalled to find that Africans were still being captured and sold into slavery in the USA.

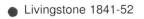
● Livingstone 1841-52
● Livingstone 1852-6

DAVID LIVINGSTONE was born in Blantyre, Scotland, in 1813. He started working in a cotton mill at the age of ten. He continued his studies at night and in 1836 got a place at medical school in Glasgow.

HENRY MORTON STANLEY was born in Wales in 1841. At the age of five he was sent to the workhouse. He left when he was fifteen and sailed as a cabin boy to New Orleans in the USA. He worked in a shop until 1862.

LIVINGSTONE took his family on expedition in 1851. They went by cart to the rivers north of Lake Ngami. When he saw the Zambezi River, Livingstone wanted to explore its whole length. Realizing this would take a long time, he sent his family back to Britain in April 1852.

IN FEBRUARY 1844, while he was living alone and working as a missionary in Mabotsa, Livingstone was attacked by a lion. His arm was badly mauled and, as he was the only doctor for hundreds of miles, he had to operate on it himself to make sure it healed.

Victoria Falls.

ON NOVEMBER, 16 1855 Livingstone became the first European to see the mighty waterfalls on the Zambezi River. He called them Victoria Falls in honor of Britain's Queen. The African name, *Mosi-oa-tunya*, is more appropriate as it means "the smoke that thunders".

STANLEY FOUGHT in the American Civil War on the Confederate side, but was taken prisoner in his first battle. He joined the Union side in exchange for freedom, but was too ill to fight. He went to sea for a while, before becoming a journalist and traveling west to look for adventure.

Livingstone's Expeditions 1858-73

After two months in Quelimane, Livingstone returned to Britain. He spent a year planning a trip on which he hoped to travel up the Zambezi in a steamboat and set up a trading center in the middle of Africa. But he did not realize that there were many rapids along the lower parts of the river. He set out in early 1858 but the steamboat could not get far upstream. He then explored overland around the Shire River and Lake Nyasa (now Lake Malawi). In 1861 he persuaded some missionaries to come out from Britain. They brought a second steamboat, but it was too big to travel as far as Lake Nyasa. Livingstone explored the area until January 1862 when a third steamboat arrived. This was also a failure and in 1863 he sold it to an Indian merchant and returned to Britain.

In late 1865 he returned to Africa with two goals: to check Speke's report on the source of the Nile, and to campaign against the ongoing slave trade. He left Zanzibar in January 1866 and spent the next seven years exploring overland around Lake Tanganyika and the Lualaba River.

LIVINGSTONE'S first steamboat was the *Ma Robert*, which could carry 36 passengers. At first it made slow but steady progress along the Zambezi River, but then it ran into rapids which it could not pass.

MARY LIVINGSTONE arrived back in Africa to join her husband's expedition in January 1862. Although she had been brought up in Africa, she became ill with malaria in April and died suddenly, in spite of treatment from a doctor.

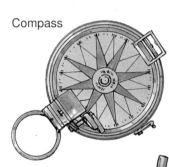

Compass

Magnifying glass

Pen

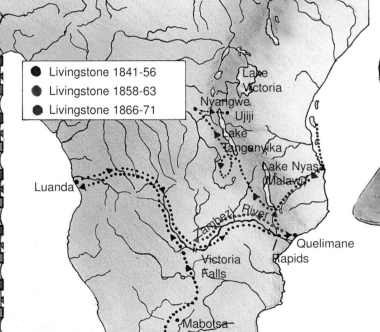

- ● Livingstone 1841-56
- ● Livingstone 1858-63
- ● Livingstone 1866-71

Lake Victoria
Nyangwe
Ujiji
Lake Tanganyika
Lake Nyasa (Malawi)
Luanda
Zambezi River
Quelimane
Victoria Falls
Rapids
Mabotsa
Kuruman

THIS MAP shows Livingstone's travels in Africa between 1841 and 1873. Many of the Europeans on his 1858 expedition died of disease while they were in Africa and the whole expedition was a failure.

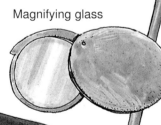

Cap

SOME OF LIVINGSTONE'S equipment survived his travels, including a compass, a pen, a magnifying glass and his blue cap. Right up to his death, he kept a journal with careful notes on everything he saw and how far he had traveled. He also wrote an account of the daily temperature, air pressure, rainfall and cloud conditions.

Massacre at Nyangwe.

ON JULY 15, 1871 Livingstone saw Arab slave traders kill over 400 Africans, mostly women and children, in Nyangwe. This upset him greatly and he became more determined to set up new trade links to replace slavery. He thought that if the Africans learned how to grow cotton in their own country it could be exported to Europe.

TRAVELING on the river was often quicker and easier than traveling overland. But there were still many dangers. On one occasion Livingstone's boat was overturned by a hippopotamus and he lost a lot of his equipment.

LIVINGSTONE took these slave chains back to Britain as proof that Africans were still being captured and sold into slavery. He believed that if the slave trade was abolished more Africans would convert to Christianity.

Livingstone and Stanley, 1871-3

By 1871 no one had heard any news of Livingstone for three years. Rumors began to spread that he was dead, or at least lost. The editor of the *New York Herald* sent his European correspondent to look for him. This was Henry Stanley who had first been to Africa in 1867 as a war reporter in Abyssinia (present-day Ethiopia).

Livingstone was at Ujiji by Lake Tanganyika, but he was ill and running out of supplies. Stanley met up with him on November 10, 1871 and stayed for several months. They explored the area around the lake and decided that it was not the source of the River Nile as Burton had thought (*see page 30*). They separated at Kazeh in March 1872 and Stanley went back to England to write his story for the newspaper.

The story made Stanley famous, but he was an adventurous and ambitious man and now wanted more excitement in his life. His chance came after Livingstone's death in May 1873. The old explorer was given a state funeral at Westminster Abbey in April 1874 and this inspired two newspapers to sponsor an expedition to Africa to continue his work. Stanley was the person they chose to lead it.

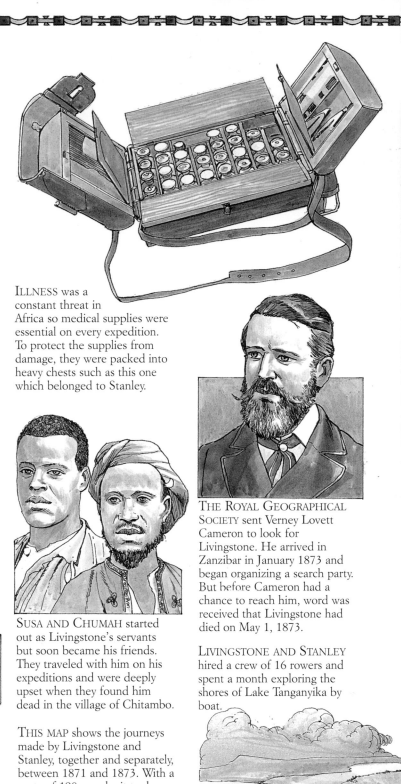

ILLNESS was a constant threat in Africa so medical supplies were essential on every expedition. To protect the supplies from damage, they were packed into heavy chests such as this one which belonged to Stanley.

THE ROYAL GEOGRAPHICAL SOCIETY sent Verney Lovett Cameron to look for Livingstone. He arrived in Zanzibar in January 1873 and began organizing a search party. But before Cameron had a chance to reach him, word was received that Livingstone had died on May 1, 1873.

LIVINGSTONE AND STANLEY hired a crew of 16 rowers and spent a month exploring the shores of Lake Tanganyika by boat.

SUSA AND CHUMAH started out as Livingstone's servants but soon became his friends. They traveled with him on his expeditions and were deeply upset when they found him dead in the village of Chitambo.

THIS MAP shows the journeys made by Livingstone and Stanley, together and separately, between 1871 and 1873. With a party of 190 people, it took Stanley 411 days to cover the 2,200 miles from Zanzibar to Ujiji.

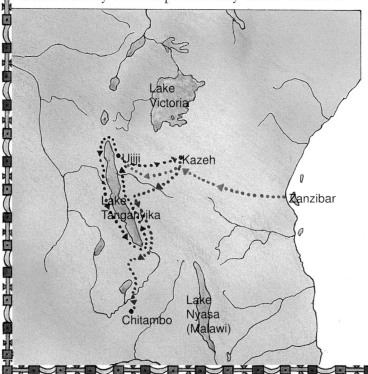

● Stanley

● Livingstone and Stanley

● Livingstone

Livingstone and Stanley meet.

WHEN LIVINGSTONE saw Stanley approaching, he commented, "This must be a luxurious traveller, and not one at his wits' end like me." Stanley greeted him with the now famous words, "Dr. Livingstone, I presume?"

BY THE TIME Stanley met him, Livingstone was already frail and weak. But he refused to return to England. Instead, he kept on looking for the source of the River Nile. Sometimes he was so exhausted that he had to be carried.

AFTER LIVINGSTONE'S DEATH at Chitambo village, Susa and Chumah preserved his body in salt and alcohol. Then, together with Jacob Wainwright who is shown here with the coffin, they made the 1,240 mile journey to Zanzibar so that the body could be shipped back to England.

Stanley's Expeditions 1874-84

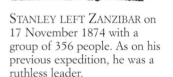

When Stanley's expedition left Zanzibar, it was the biggest ever organized up to that time. He planned to march overland until he found the Lualaba River, then follow it down to the Atlantic coast. He took with him a collapsible boat which he assembled at Lake Victoria. After exploring the lake, he went overland to Ujiji from where he explored Lake Tanganyika. He then made his way to Nyangwe which was near to the Lualaba River. There he was able to hire 500 more porters and some armed men from local chiefs and Arab slave traders to replace the ones who had deserted him.

From Nyangwe Stanley set off down the Lualaba River, which, as he had thought, turned west and flowed into the Congo (now the Zaire). By the time he reached Boma, he claimed to have fought 32 battles and to have destroyed 80 settlements whose inhabitants opposed him.

In 1879 the Belgian king, Leopold II, hired him to go back to Africa and help him establish an

STANLEY LEFT ZANZIBAR on 17 November 1874 with a group of 356 people. As on his previous expedition, he was a ruthless leader.

BY THE TIME he reached Lake Victoria he had only 166 people left. Most of the others had deserted, but some had died from disease and exhaustion.

overseas empire on the Congo River. Stanley did this between 1879 and 1884. As he was claiming the south bank, however, the French were exploring and settling along the north. What became known as the "Scramble for Africa" had begun.

SOME AFRICANS were friendly towards Stanley and his group, but many more thought that they were slave traders on a raid. As a result, the locals often attacked Stanley's boats as they approached. Stanley fought back using guns.

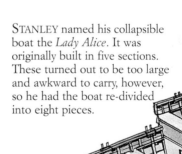

STANLEY named his collapsible boat the *Lady Alice*. It was originally built in five sections. These turned out to be too large and awkward to carry, however, so he had the boat re-divided into eight pieces.

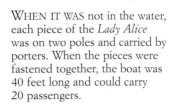

WHEN IT WAS not in the water, each piece of the *Lady Alice* was on two poles and carried by porters. When the pieces were fastened together, the boat was 40 feet long and could carry 20 passengers.

● Stanley 1871
● ● Livingstone and
● Stanley 1871
● Livingstone 1872-3
● Stanley 1874-7

THIS MAP shows Stanley's route from Zanzibar to Boma. It took from November 14, 1874 to August 9, 1877. At times the temperature reached 104° F and much of the journey was through dense rainforest.

STANLEY was a harsh leader and did not hesitate to use force to make people obey him. Here he can be seen threatening to shoot a porter if he drops the box he is carrying on his head across the river.

IN JANUARY 1877 Stanley's party arrived at a series of seven waterfalls which he named the Stanley Falls, even though they were already called the Boyoma Falls. Several men drowned here.

The Stanley Falls.

Mary Kingsley

Most of the explorers who went to Africa were men. However, a few women went there, too. They included May Sheldon, who led an expedition to Mount Kilimanjaro, and Alexine Tinne who explored the Nile to the south of Khartoum. But the most famous of them was Mary Kingsley, who explored West and Equatorial Africa in the 1890s.

She had led a quiet life until she was 30. She was self-educated and had a little money, so, when her parents died, she decided to visit West Africa. On her first visit she traveled along the coast from Cabinda to the mouth of the Congo, where she collected specimens for the British Museum. Her second visit was mainly to what is now Gabon. She spent time with the Fang people who lived along the Ogowe River. They were said to be cannibals, but she lived safely among them. She studied their culture and decided that they were worth protecting from European influences. She also realized that the Africans were not wicked savages in need of religion as the missionaries claimed. This view made her almost unique in Victorian England.

MARY KINGSLEY was born in London, England, in 1862. Back in Britain, she gave many talks about her travels and became an adviser to the minister for the colonies. She died in 1900 in South Africa while working as a nurse during the Boer War.

FROM HER TRAVELS, Kingsley brought back 65 different species of fish and 18 different species of reptile. They included the snoutfish (*right*) which she preserved in alcohol and the fish (*below*) which were named after her.

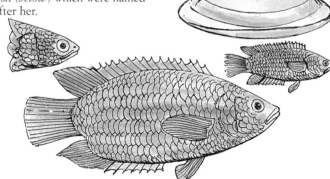

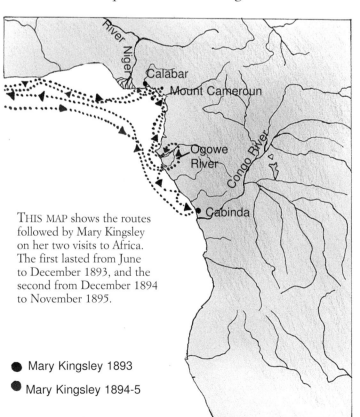

THIS MAP shows the routes followed by Mary Kingsley on her two visits to Africa. The first lasted from June to December 1893, and the second from December 1894 to November 1895.

● Mary Kingsley 1893

● Mary Kingsley 1894-5

AT THE END of her second visit to Africa, Kingsley climbed Mount Cameroun, an active volcano, some 13,500 feet high. When she reached the top, she marked the occasion by leaving her visiting card under a stone.

Mary Kingsley fights off a crocodile.

KINGSLEY was often in danger and had many narrow escapes, which she later wrote about in her book, *Travels in West Africa*. When a crocodile tried to climb into her canoe, she scared it off with "a clip on the snout with a paddle", then paddled quickly to deeper water where it could not follow her.

KINGSLEY had very little money to spare so she paid her way by trading colored handkerchiefs, tobacco, pocket-knives and metal fish-hooks for items such as this carved wooden head of a Fang girl, which she gave to the British Museum.

A FANG VILLAGE had a row of houses at each side of a single street. Both ends of the street were blocked by guardhouses to protect the inhabitants from attack by other people or wild animals. Vegetables were grown on small clearings around the village. When the soil became exhausted, the people moved on and built another village somewhere else.

Towards Independence

The "Scramble for Africa" started around 1880 and lasted until around 1900. During this period a different type of explorer went to the continent. Often heavily armed and sponsored by their governments, they claimed vast areas of land on behalf of various European rulers who wanted to set up overseas empires. These empires would provide raw materials for European industries and a ready market for European goods.

As they drew new borders on the map, Europeans had little regard for the peoples of Africa or for their traditional way of life. All resistance to the new regimes was quickly squashed by well-equipped armies from Europe, and thousands of Africans were killed. Farmers were forced to grow crops such as tea, coffee and cotton for export to Europe, instead of just growing food for their families as they had done in the past. Vast areas of rainforest were destroyed for their timber and to clear new land for agriculture, with little thought given to the long-term damage this might do to the environment.

LEOPOLD II was king of Belgium from 1865 to 1909. In 1885 he established rule over the Congo Free State. In 1908 this became known as the Belgian Congo. It regained its independence in 1960 and has been called Zaire since 1965.

PIERRE SAVORGNAN DE BRAZZA (1852-1905) was a French explorer. He served in the French Navy and in 1878 he led an expedition to explore and colonize what became known as French Equatorial Africa. It is now part of Zaire.

MANY EUROPEANS exploited the land and the peoples of Africa. Hunters killed thousands of animals – many to the point of extinction – for sport.

JEAN BAPTISTE MARCHAND (1863-1934) was a French soldier. In July 1898 he tried to claim Fashoda (now Kodok) for France. This led to a crisis between France and Britain and he had to leave Africa.

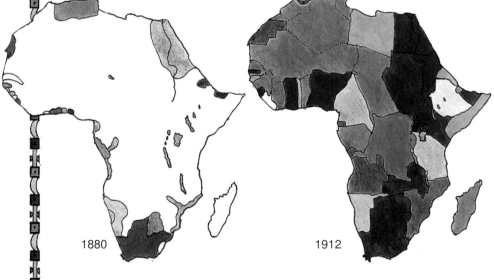

1880

1912

IN 1880 the European nations ruled less than five percent of Africa, but by 1900 they ruled the whole continent apart from Ethiopia and Liberia.

- French
- British
- British Independent
- German
- Spanish
- Portuguese
- Belgian
- Italian
- Independent
- Boer

A SELECTION OF AFRICAN COUNTRIES and the colonial government in place at the time of their independence:

MOROCCO	France	1956
TUNISIA	France	1956
GHANA	Britain	1957
NIGER	France	1960
IVORY COAST	France	1960
BENIN	France	1960
NIGERIA	Britain	1960
CAMEROON	France	1960
ZAIRE	Belgium	1960
SOMALIA	Italy/France	1960
SENEGAL	France	1960
THE GAMBIA	Britain	1960
SIERRA LEONE	Britain	1961
ALGERIA	France	1962
UGANDA	Britain	1962
KENYA	Britain	1963
ZAMBIA	Britain	1964
MOZAMBIQUE	Portugal	1975
ANGOLA	Portugal	1975
DJIBOUTI	France	1977
ZIMBABWE	Britain	1980

Mizon in the Congo.

After World War II, the situation changed slowly. Many realized that people should have the right to choose who governed their own country rather than have laws forced on them by foreigners. As a result, the countries of Africa have gradually regained their independence over the last 50 years. But in many places this did not happen peacefully because rival African groups struggled for power, or foreign inhabitants tried to keep control.

EXPLORERS like Lieutenant Louis Mizon helped France to gain the largest share of colonies in Africa. They covered almost a third of Africa from Algeria in the north to Gabon in the south. France also claimed the island of Madagascar in the Indian Ocean.

CECIL RHODES (1853-1902) was a South African politician of British descent. He wanted to expand British rule along the full length of Africa, from Cairo to Cape Town. He took control of the lands of the Ndebele and Shona peoples, and renamed them Rhodesia (now Zimbabwe).

JOMO KENYATTA (*above*) was sworn in as the first president of Kenya when the country regained its independence from Britain in 1962. Thirty years later, only the Republic of South Africa had a white government.

IN SOUTH AFRICA a system known as apartheid prevented black South Africans voting. When this was abolished, elections were held and in April 1994 Nelson Mandela became president of his country.

TIME CHART

BC

814 The Phoenicians set up a trading center at Carthage on the North African coast.

450 Hanno, a Phoenician, leads a fleet of 67 ships around the coast of Africa to the Gulf of Guinea. The knowledge of iron-working spreads south of the Sahara Desert.

440 Herodotus, the Greek historian, visits Egypt and writes about the River Nile.

30 The Romans conquer Egypt.

AD

c100 Bantu speakers start spreading south and east from what is now Nigeria. They take with them the knowledge of iron-working and farming.

350 Ethiopia converts to Christianity.

500 Bantu speakers reach the south of Africa.

642 The Arabs conquer Egypt and start to convert the people of North Africa to Islam.

1100 Almost the whole of North Africa is converted to Islam by this date.

1304 The Arab traveler Ibn Battuta is born.

1415 Prince Henry (also known as Henry the Navigator) captures the town of Ceuta in North Africa for the Portuguese.

1418 Prince Henry sends out his first expedition. It reaches the island of Madeira.

1434 The Portuguese sailor Gil Eanes sails beyond Cape Bojador and returns safely.

1441 A Portuguese ship brings back the first gold and slaves from West Africa.

1448 Prince Henry sets up the first Portuguese trading post on Arguin Island near Cape Blanco.

1482 The Portuguese sailor Diogo Cao reaches the mouth of the Zaire River.

1485 Diogo Cao reaches Cape Cross in what is now Namibia.

1488 Bartolomeu Dias becomes the first European to sail into the Indian Ocean.

1498 Vasco da Gama reaches Calicut in India.

1500 Pedro Alvarez Cabral sails from Portugal to India, via Brazil and South Africa.

1502 By use of force Vasco da Gama sets up trading links between Portugal, East Africa and India.

1652	The Dutch set up a colony in Cape Town, to supply their ships going to India and the East Indies.
1768	James Bruce sets out from Alexandria, Egypt, to look for the source of the River Nile.
1788	In London, Joseph Banks sets up the Association for Promoting the Discovery of the Interior Parts of Africa.
1790	James Bruce publishes his book, *Travels to Discover the Source of the Nile*.
1795	Mungo Park sets out to explore the Niger.
1805	Mungo Park arrives in Gambia to lead a second expedition along the Niger. It ends when he drowns at Bussa Falls in 1806.
1820	The French explorer, Frederic Cailliaud, joins an expedition sent out by the Viceroy of Egypt to find the source of the Nile. The expedition reaches Gondokoro before turning back.
1826	Alexander Laing becomes the first European to reach Timbuktu, but is murdered on his return journey.
1828	René-August Caillié becomes the first European to reach Timbuktu and come back alive.
1841	David Livingstone arrives in South Africa to work as a missionary.
1845	James Richardson travels overland from Tripoli on the Mediterranean coast to the oases of Ghudamis and Ghat in the Sahara Desert on behalf of the British Bible Society.
1848	Livingstone goes on an expedition across the Kalahari Desert.
1850	Richardson leads a second expedition, accompanied by Heinrich Barth. They reach Lake Chad then split up. Richardson dies of malaria, but Barth goes on to Timbuktu, arriving there in 1853.
1852-6	Livingstone crosses Africa, following the Zambezi River.
1855	Richard Burton and John Speke make their first attempt at finding the source of the River Nile.

1857	Burton and Speke set out on a second expedition to find the source of the Nile.
1858	Burton and Speke are the first Europeans to see Lake Tanganyika. Speke reaches Lake Nyanza and renames it Lake Victoria. He is convinced this is the source of the Nile. Burton argues that the source of the Nile is a river flowing from Lake Tanganyika.
1860	Speke leads another expedition to Africa, this time with James Grant. They explore Lake Victoria.
1866	Livingstone sets out to investigate Speke's claim and look for the source of the Nile.
1871	Henry Stanley sets out to look for Livingstone. He finds him at Ujiji on Lake Tanganyika. They explore the area and decide that it is not the source of the Nile as Burton had thought.

1873	Livingstone dies in Africa.
1874	Stanley sets out to explore the Lualaba River.
1879	The Belgian king, Leopold II, hires Stanley to go back to Africa and help him to establish an overseas empire.
1880	The "Scramble for Africa" begins as European countries divide the continent amongst themselves with little regard for the people, the environment or any natural boundaries.
1893	Mary Kingsley makes her first visit to Africa.
1894	Mary Kingsley makes her second visit to Africa.

GLOSSARY

The American Civil War began in 1861. The northern states (the Union) were against slavery and fought against the southern states (the Confederacy) which wanted to keep slavery. In 1865 the south surrendered and slavery was abolished.

Apartheid
laws used in South Africa from 1948 to 1993 which forced black people to live in separate areas from white people and deprived them of most of their human rights, including the right to vote in elections. Many of the laws were abolished in 1990-1 and in 1993 black people were finally given the right to vote.

Artifact
any object made by humans.

Ashanti
a former kingdom in what is now southern Ghana.

Astronomer
a scientist who studies the stars and planets.

Black Death
a disease which swept Europe in 1347-8. It was carried by rat fleas and was very infectious.

Boer Wars
two wars in South Africa between the British and the Boers (also known as Afrikaners) who were of Dutch descent. The first lasted from 1880 to 1881 and the second from 1899 to 1902. In the second war the Boers were defeated and the British took control of the country.

Botanist
a scientist who studies plants and flowers.

British East India Company
a company set up in

1600 to deal in spices from the East Indies. In the 18th century the East India Company had a lot of power in India. This power was gradually taken over by the British government and the company ceased to exist in 1873.

Brocade
silk cloth with a raised pattern woven into it.

Caravan
a group of people, usually with camels, traveling together for safety reasons.

Cereal crop
plants such as wheat, barley, corn and oats whose grains (or seeds) can be eaten by humans.

Colony
a group of people from one country who make a permanent settlement in another country.

Dysentery
a disease of the intestines, often resulting in fever and pain.

Emissary
someone who is sent out on a mission.

Hottentots
the European name for the Khoikhoi people of southern Africa who lived by herding, hunting and gathering until most of their lands were taken from them gradually by European settlers.

Jesuit
a member of the Society of Jesus, founded by St Ignatius Loyola in 1533, to spread the Roman Catholic religion.

Koran
the holy book of the Islamic religion.

Latitude
the distance of a place north or south of the Equator.

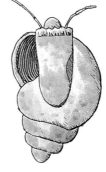

Malaria
a feverish disease caused by mosquito bites.

Missionary
someone who tries to spread their religion among other people, usually in a foreign country.

Monsoon wind
a wind in the Indian Ocean. Between April and October it blows from the south-west, but from November to March it blows from the north-east.

Mosque
place where Muslims go to pray.

Ottoman Empire
an Islamic empire, based in Turkey. It was at its most powerful in the 15th and 16th centuries.

Phoenicians
people from the area known as Phoenicia (now in Lebanon and Syria). They flourished between 1000 BC and 200 BC.

Pilot
someone who guides ships through difficult waters or into harbors.

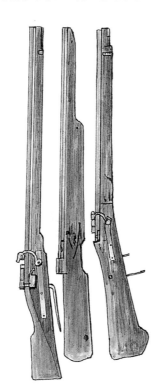

Plantation
a large estate where crops such as cotton, tobacco and sugar are grown.

Porcelain
very fine pottery with a hard and shiny glaze.

Porter
someone who is employed to carry luggage on a journey.

Punjab
a hot, dry region now in India and Pakistan.

Rapids
a place on the river where the current is very fast and strong.

Scurvy
a weakening disease caused by a lack of vitamins in the diet.

Sextant
an instrument used for measuring angles in navigation and surveying.

Sleeping sickness
a disease which causes extreme fatigue in people and animals.

Songhai
a West African people, living in the region of the River Niger to the south of Timbuktu.

Tuaregs
semi-nomadic peoples who live in and around the Sahara Desert. In the 19th century they raided trade caravans and attacked travelers.

Viceroy
a person who rules in a colony on behalf of the king or queen of another country.

Visiting card
a card printed with a person's name and address, and a message. Middle-class Victorians usually left them if they visited a house and found nobody at home.

Workhouse
a 19th-century British institution where the poor, the unemployed and the old were given food and shelter in exchange for hard work.

Zoologist
a scientist who studies animals.